W9-CEO-465

PERIMETER, AREA, and VOLUME

A Monster Book of Dimensions

by David A. Adler • illustrated by Edward Miller

Holiday House / New York

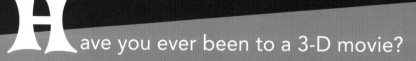

Have you ever been to a 3-D movie?

3-D movies look real. If there's a monster walking on the screen, it might seem as if he is walking toward you. As the monster on the screen gets bigger and bigger, it seems as if he's coming closer and closer.

Such movies are called **3-D** because they seem to have **three dimensions**. They seem to have **length**, **width**, and **depth**.

The three dimensions are sometimes called by **different names**. We might say something is **tall**, **high**, or **long**; **wide** or **broad**; **deep** or **thick**. Whatever words we use, all things we can hold or walk around have **three dimensions**.

Here are the monster stars of the movie *Monsters in the Neighborhood*. They're posing for a picture. Are they all the same size?

Some might be the same height but not the same size. **Height** is just one dimension. Each monster has three dimensions.

Each monster is tall or short.

Each monster is wide or narrow.

Each monster is fat or thin.

To know how big something really is you need to know all three dimensions. But sometimes you need to know just one dimension.

In the movie *Monsters in the Neighborhood*, the monsters are bothered by nosy neighbors who run across their yards and look in their windows. The monsters decide to put up fences.

ACTION!

Ding Dong!

Monster Movie
Scene 1

Before they can buy the fences, they need to know how long each side must be. They need to know the total length of the fence around each yard. **Length** is just one dimension.

Take a look at these two yards. One is bigger than the other. How much fencing would the monsters need for each yard? To find out, add up the lengths of all the sides. When you add up the sides of each yard, you are finding its **perimeter**— the distance around.

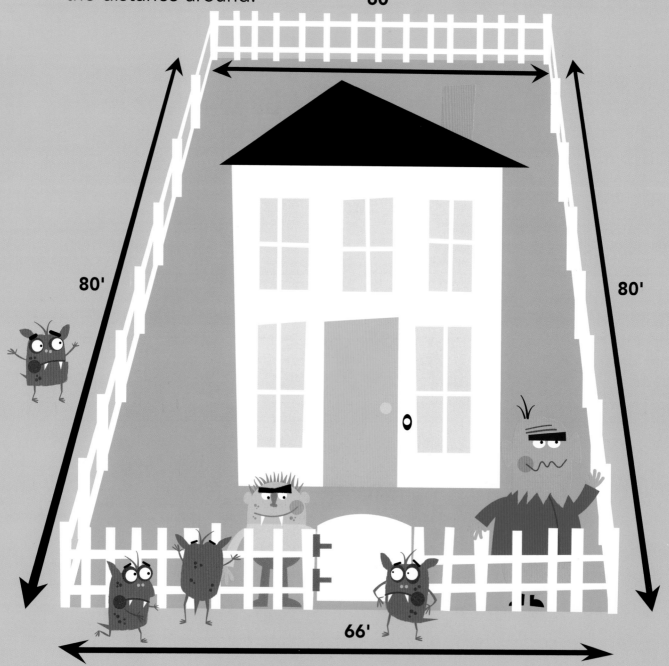

60' + 80' + 66' + 80' = 286'

1 foot = 0.3 meter

' means foot or feet

40'

90'

90'

42'

40' + 90' + 42' + 90' = 262'

The distance around a circle is its **circumference**.
To find the circumference of a circle, you first measure its
radius, the length of a straight line drawn from any point
on the edge of the circle to its center. Then you double its
radius and multiply that by pi (π), which is about 3.14.

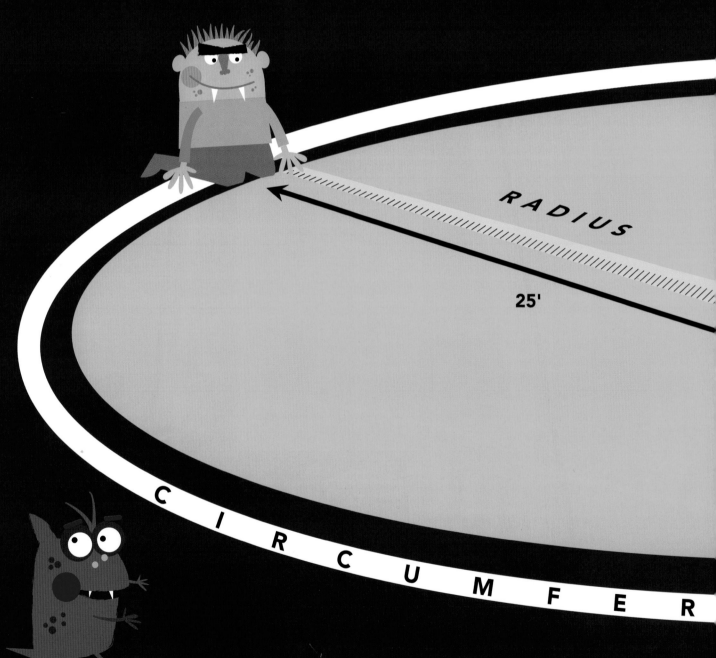

RADIUS

25'

CIRCUMFER

Inches, feet, miles, centimeters, meters, and kilometers each measure just one dimension.

25" x 2" x 3.14 = 157"

E   N   C   E

" means inch or inches

Look at the posters outside the movie theater. Each has a drawing of a monster. Do the monsters in the posters look real?

It's difficult to make a drawing look completely real because real things have three dimensions and a picture has **two dimensions**. Pictures have just length and width.

Pictures and the surfaces of flat objects have two dimensions.

MONSTERS IN THE NEIGHBORHOOD

IN 3-D

STARRING

FRANCIS STEIN

TICKET

With paper and crayons, draw a picture of a monster. Does it look real?

How big is the movie screen?

If the side of each square is 1 foot long by 1 foot wide, the **area** of the square is 1 square foot. Count the squares. You are finding the area of the screen.

Look again at the screen. It's a rectangle. It has four straight sides. Its opposite sides are the same size, and all four angles are right angles. To find the area of a rectangle, you multiply its length by its width. The length of the movie screen is 12 feet. Its width is 16 feet. Its area is 12' x 16'. Its area is 192 square feet.

16'

12'

area

12' x 16' = 192 square feet

Area measures surface. It's a two-dimensional measure.

Get a ruler or tape measure. Measure the area of this page. It's 10 inches long and 8 inches wide. To find the area of this page, multiply the length by the width.

Square inches, square feet, square miles, square centimeters, square meters, and square kilometers each measure area.

1 square inch is about 6.45 square centimeters

(Answer: The area of the page is 80 square inches.)

This book has three dimensions. The very top of this page to the bottom is the book's **length**. The left side of this page to its right side is the book's **width**. When you close this book and look at the pile of pages all bound together, you are looking at the book's third dimension, its **depth**, or thickness.

At the movies, you can buy a large box of popcorn or a jumbo box. Which box is bigger? That's easy. The jumbo box is bigger.

What makes one box bigger than the other? One box is bigger than the other because it's higher, wider, or thicker. When any one of the three dimensions increases, the size of the box increases. Of course, when both boxes are filled, the jumbo popcorn box has more popcorn in it than the large box.

We call the amount a box holds, or the space anything with three dimensions takes up, its **volume**. The larger the box, the greater its volume.

The jumbo box is 8 inches high, 6 inches wide, and 4 inches deep. To find its volume, multiply 8 by 6 by 4.

The volume of the jumbo box is 192 cubic inches.

The large box is 6 inches high, 4 inches wide, and 3 inches deep. To find its volume, multiply 6 by 4 by 3.

The volume of the large box is 72 cubic inches.

You can compare the volume of many boxes by measuring the three dimensions of each and then multiplying.

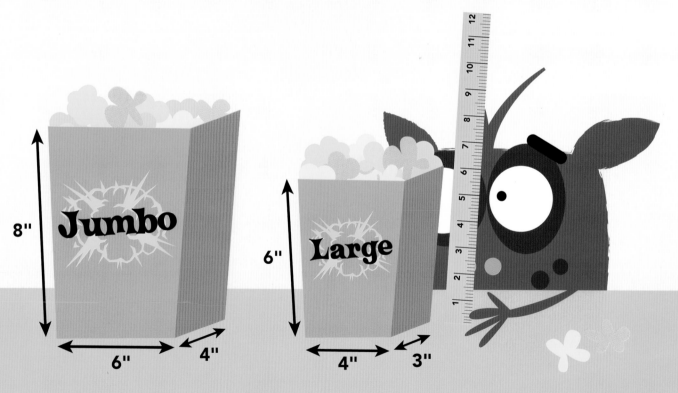

8"

Jumbo

6"   4"

6"

Large

4"   3"

8" x 6" x 4" = 192 cubic inches   6" x 4" x 3" = 72 cubic inches

1 cubic inch = 16.39 cubic centimeters

A cube has three dimensions: height, width, and depth, so we measure volume in **cubic measures**. A **cubic inch** is a cube that is 1 inch high, 1 inch wide, and 1 inch deep. A **cubic centimeter** is a cube that is 1 centimeter high, 1 centimeter wide, and 1 centimeter deep.

Cubic inches, cubic feet, cubic centimeters, and cubic meters each measure volume.

Tonight is the opening night of *Monsters in the Neighborhood*. The monster stars and their families have come to the premiere.

It's time for pictures! The photographer tells the monsters and their families to line up. He wants short monsters in front and tall monsters in back. In lining up the monsters, the photographer is only interested in **one dimension**. He's only interested in the height of the monsters.

HEIGHT

It's starting to rain!

The photographer puts away his camera. The monsters rush to get inside. But the door is not made for monsters. Some of them are too tall to get through. Some are too wide to get through.

The door frame has two dimensions. It has height and width.

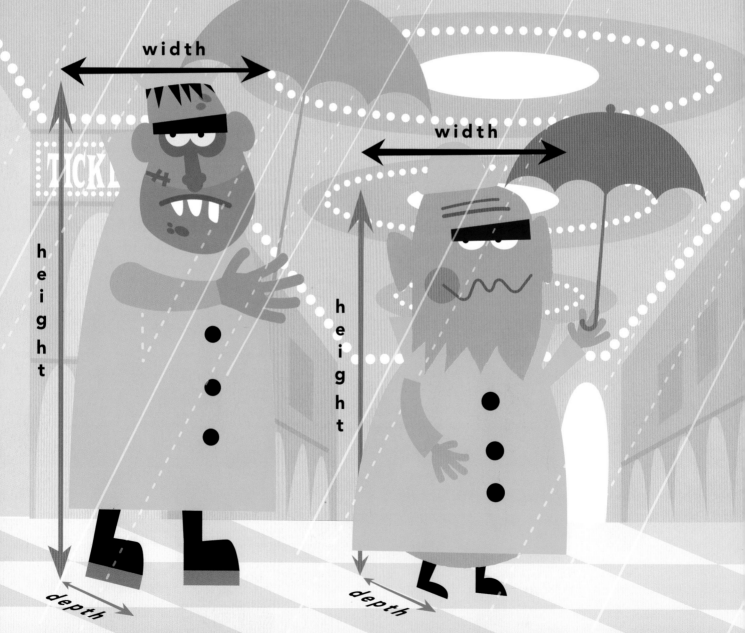

Now it's time to go home. But it's still raining.

There are lots of raincoats in lots of sizes. The biggest monster will need the biggest raincoat. The size of each monster is determined by how tall or short, how wide or narrow, and how fat or thin the monster is.

width

height

depth

width

height

depth

width

height

depth

Perimeter and **circumference** are the distances around one-dimensional shapes. **Area** is the space inside a two-dimensional object. **Volume** is the space a three-dimensional object contains. Monsters and everything you can hold, pick up, or walk around have **three dimensions**.

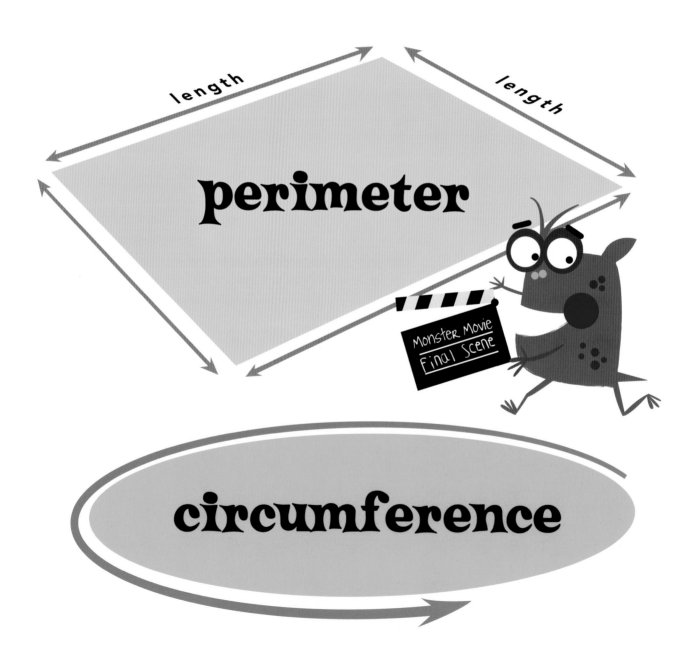

length

length

perimeter

Monster Movie
Final Scene

circumference

width

length

area

height

volume

width

depth

For Kate and John,
many thanks
—D. A. A.

The publisher would like to thank Grace Wilkie for reviewing this book for accuracy. Grace is the Past President of the Association of Mathematics Teachers of New York State and New York State Mathematics Honor Society as well as an expert on Common Core Standards, National Council of Teachers of Mathematics Standards, and New York State Mathematics Standards.

Text copyright © 2012 by David A. Adler
Illustrations copyright © 2012 by Edward Miller III
All Rights Reserved
HOLIDAY HOUSE is registered in the U.S. Patent and Trademark Office.
Printed and Bound in November 2011 at Tien Wah Press,
Johor Bahru, Johor, Malaysia.
The text typeface is Avenir.
www.holidayhouse.com
First Edition
1 3 5 7 9 10 8 6 4 2

Library of Congress Cataloging-in-Publication Data
Adler, David A.
Perimeter, area, and volume : a monster book of dimensions /
by David A. Adler ; illustrated by Edward Miller. — 1st ed.
p. cm.
ISBN 978-0-8234-2290-6 (hardcover)
1. Weights and measures—Juvenile literature.
2. Dimensions—Juvenile literature. I. Miller, Edward, 1964- ill. II. Title.
QC90.6.A35 2012
516'.15—dc22
2010048653

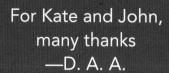

Visit **www.davidaadler.com** for more information on the author, for a list of his books, and to download teacher's guides and educational materials. You can also learn more about the writing process, take fun quizzes, and read select pages from David A. Adler's books.

Visit **www.edmiller.com** for more information on the illustrator and a list of his books.
Become a fan of **Edward Miller Designs** on **Facebook**.

516.
15
A

Adler, David A.

Perimeter, area,
and volume

DUE DATE   MCN   02/12   16.95